*Stories About What's Important In Life*
*Inspiring Book for Kids about Values, Emotions, and Relationships*
*to Boost Essential Social-Emotional Skills*

**Written by** Sophia Anna Ritter
**Illustrations by** Tatiana Hrynenko
**Production management by** Magdalene Ward

This book is a work of fiction. Characters and events in this novel are the product of the author's imagination. Any similarity to persons living or dead is purely coincidental.

For information address LittleBigPage, 312 W. 2nd St #1934
Casper, WY 82601, United States.

Paperback ISBN: 9788367973137

First Edition

# STORIES ABOUT WHAT'S IMPORTANT IN LIFE

SOPHIA A. RITTER

You can **download the free audiobook** version of this book.
Go to the *last page* for more information!

# contents

MOM

Gamma
(GRANDMA)

Bubba

Oscar

DAD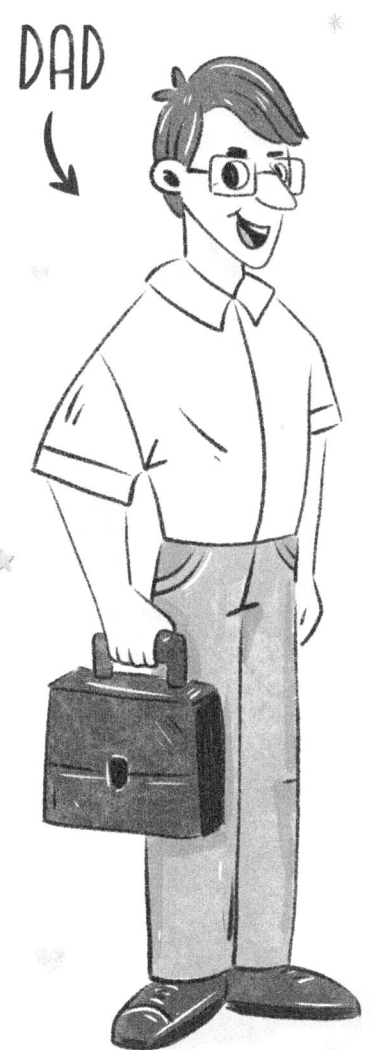

EMMA

JOSEPHINE

LUNA

# Introduction

Want to know a secret?

What if I told you magic is not just in fairy tales? What if I told you it lives within us too? The magic of love, hope, friendship, kindness—the list goes on.

Welcome to *Stories about What's Important in Life*. Here, ten enchanting chapters eagerly await you. Each one teaches a valuable lesson that will make your heart sparkle!

Are you ready to embark on an extraordinary journey? Imagine a world where everyone treats each other with kindness. A place where respect is the golden rule and love fills the air. Have you ever wondered how this world would look and feel? What if I said that YOU have the power to create this magical world NOW?

Sometimes, life can be a bit confusing. You might feel like you're not sure how to handle certain situations. Or maybe you don't know how to show love and kindness.

Don't worry, my friend. We've all been there. That's why this book is here—to help you. Together, we'll go on adventures of the heart and find the amazing benefits that await you.

Each chapter will be a ride. A ride where you get to meet all the different emotions you feel. Take a few minutes to understand them. And at the end of every ride, there will be a surprise waiting for you. A set of questions that will show how attentive you've been the whole time.

Now, you might be wondering, who am I to guide you on this extraordinary adventure? Well, dear reader, let me introduce myself. I am Sophia, a dedicated explorer of the human heart. I have spent years studying and understanding the secrets of what makes a heart magical. But most importantly, I know how we can make our hearts magical too.

Are you ready to discover the wonders that lie within you? If so, turn the page and embark on Chapter One.

Remember, my young adventurer, this magical journey begins with you!

## CHAPTER ONE

# Sticking with Love

Emma stepped off the school bus and made her way home. The hope to have her favorite snack increased with every step. She bounced through the front door, her backpack slung over her right shoulder. As she did, she breathed in the familiar scent of home. It was the smell of warm and gooey chocolate chip cookies. The first thought that popped into her mind was *love*.

Setting her backpack down, Emma began rummaging through it.

"Where is it?!" she muttered, flinging her coloring book from the bag. "Aha!"

Emma could practically hear angels singing in the background. Slowly, she took out the glorious, shining sticker sheets. What resulted was nothing short of a *love storm*.

Emma began sticking hearts on anything and everything she *loved*. She placed one on the door.

"I love coming home from school!"

She placed a sticker on the fluffy purple carpet. Then she stuck some on the window, the mirror she'd bought with her mom, and the fresh flowers her dad had placed in the vase this morning.

"I love this and this and this..."

She twirled around, feeling like the most loving person ever. Emma was so caught up in her excitement that she almost didn't notice Oscar walk in behind her.

Oscar was a daring adventurer. Yet, like most older brothers, Oscar thought he knew more than his sister.

"What the...?" He paused, eyeing the stickers everywhere.

"I'm putting heart stickers on everything I love!" Emma replied, sticking one on her backpack.

Oscar snorted. "Everything? That's kind of silly, don't you think? You can't love *everything.*"

Emma's face fell, and she felt a pang of disappointment in her chest. She didn't understand why Oscar had to be so mean.

"Yes, I can!" she said, trying to keep her voice from trembling. "I love our house and my toys and my dress and—"

"But you can't love a stupid piece of cloth or a mirror or a backpack," Oscar interrupted.

Emma scowled, ignoring her brother. She was determined to keep spreading love. "I can love whatever I want!" she exclaimed, sticking her tongue out at Oscar.

Oscar rolled his eyes and shook his head. He muttered something about how silly little sisters could be. But Emma didn't care. She had found something that made her happy. She wasn't going to let anyone take that from her.

Oscar moved on, leaving Emma behind. It was then that she heard her brother's excited call: "COOKIES!"

That's when Emma remembered what had first filled her with love. "Oh, I love cookies too!"

Emma skipped into the kitchen. Their mom was taking out a fresh batch of cookies from the oven.

"Mom, Mom!" Emma called. "You won't believe what we learned about today!"

She reached out to grab one of the cookies from the

cooling rack. It was still warm and chewy. The chocolate melted in her mouth, making her fall in love.

A smile instantly lit up Mom's face. "What did you learn, sweetie?" she asked, leaning in for a hug.

Emma grinned, taking a big bite before answering. "We learned about love today!"

"Love?" Mom repeated.

Oscar, who was munching on two cookies at the same time, rolled his eyes. "Not again!" He left before Mom could ask about his day.

Emma nodded, ignoring her brother. "Yeah! My teacher said there are different kinds of love, and we should always show it. She even gave us these heart stickers to put on everything we love."

Emma held up the sheet of glittery pink and red hearts. It was already half empty.

Mom chuckled at Emma's energy. "Well, what does love mean to you?" she asked.

Emma paused, taking a moment to consider her answer. "Love is like when you share your favorite toys with your best friend. It's when you make silly faces and sing off-key. It's that warm, fuzzy feeling in your heart when you see something you like," she said.

Mom smiled, nodding in agreement. "That's a very wise definition, Emma."

Emma's eyes lit up, and she grabbed another heart sticker. "I love everyone and everything, Mom! I love these cookies and my toys and my pink dress and my glitter pens and the flowers outside and the clouds in the sky and—"

Her mother laughed. "Okay, okay, I get it! You're a very loving person, Emma," she said, ruffling her daughter's hair.

Emma finished her snack, thinking of all the things she could put hearts on. She bounded through the house excitedly, her small feet barely touching the ground as she went.

With each sticker, a little burst of joy filled her chest. She placed a sticker on the fluffy fur of their cat, Luna. Giggling, she watched as Luna flicked her tail in response. She pasted one on the fridge. There, her mother had proudly hung a drawing Emma had sketched in class. She laid one on the oatmeal chocolate chip cookies and snatched up two more cookies while she was at it.

Emma went from room to room. She placed heart stickers on everything that made her feel warm and fuzzy.

She put one on her bedspread, her favorite book, and her tablet. She even placed one on the vase of flowers her mother had just brought home.

With each sticker, Emma felt like she was making a little bubble of love around her. She didn't care if Oscar thought it was silly. To her, love was something to be shared.

Moments later, Emma heard a knock on the front door. She rushed to answer it. On the other side stood her grandmother, Gamma. Emma's face lit up, and she gave Gamma a big hug. As she hugged her, she placed a heart sticker on Gamma's sweater. Emma explained the meaning behind the stickers and told Gamma she loved her fluffy sweaters.

Gamma smiled and said, "Oh, my dear, thank you."

Emma couldn't wait to show Gamma all the things she had put heart stickers on. She led Gamma through the sticker-filled house. Emma showed her everything she loved. But then, she told Gamma how Oscar thought her stickers were silly.

Gamma listened carefully to Emma and then said, "Maybe Oscar was a little jealous, or he might be feeling left out. Did he get a sticker too?"

Emma thought for a moment and then her eyes widened. She realized that she hadn't put a sticker on Oscar.

Gamma continued, "You know, Emma, you can love everything, but some things might mean more to you than others."

"Hmmmm," Emma thought about Gamma's words a bit. "Yeah, I do love Mom and Dad more than chocolate chip cookies. I even love Oscar more than my teddy..."

Emma paused at the words that had left her mouth. She loved Mom, Dad, and Oscar, of course she did.

Emma felt a pang of guilt. The thought of putting a sticker on them hadn't crossed her mind. She loved them so much that she thought it went without saying. But now she realized that she should have told them.

Immediately, Emma ran through the house. She found Oscar first. He was in the living room reading a book. She hugged him tightly and placed a heart sticker on his chest. Oscar blushed and looked surprised.

"I'm sorry, Oscar. I completely forgot to give you this," Emma said.

Oscar smiled as his cheeks turned bright red. "Yeah, yeah."

Emma beamed at her brother. She felt a warmth spread through her chest. It was different from what she felt when she put a heart sticker on any object. The warmth came from knowing that she had made her brother feel loved.

As the family sat down at the dinner table together that evening, Emma looked around. They all had stickers placed right on their hearts. She realized that her stickers didn't just show what she loved. They also reminded her of the people she loved. And that was the most important thing of all.

What do you think
is the best way
to show love?

Is it through magical words,
superhero-like actions,
or something super sneaky?

Think about someone you love,
like your awesome friend
or cool family member.

Imagine how you can show
them your love today.
Let your imagination fly!

## CHAPTER TWO

# The Great Rainy Day Quest

Oscar found himself trapped indoors on a rainy day. Gazing out the window, he frowned. The family dog, Bubba, shared his feelings. Bubba's tail sagged low, and he gazed longingly at the rainy world.

"I'm so bored!" Oscar huffed, folding his arms.

"Well, honey, why don't you play something inside?" his mom said. She was sitting on the sofa near him. "Just remember to be respectful of the rest of us in the house."

Oscar didn't pay much attention to what Mom said. His mind was already whirring with his next quest.

Oscar's thirst for adventure led him to Emma's room. There, amidst the scattered books and toys, lay a breathtaking sight. It was a diorama. His sister had been carefully crafting it for a school project.

"Wow, Bubba, look at this! Emma's made a whole little world in here," Oscar said.

Bubba wagged his tail in response, his eyes gleaming with curiosity.

The diorama was a masterpiece of popsicle sticks. It showed a play Emma had seen at the theater. Tiny figures, lovingly painted, brought the small world to life.

Oscar's eyes lit up with mischievous delight. He imagined a different use for these carefully made pieces. He plucked the tiny figures off the diorama and playfully waved them around. Bubba, sensing Oscar's excitement, joined in too.

Laughter filled the room. Oscar tossed the tiny characters to Bubba, who chased after them. The figurines became a game of fetch. Though Oscar and Bubba enjoyed their playtime, they left absolute destruction behind them in the room. The diorama lay ruined. The carefully constructed scenes were broken.

* * *

Before long, Emma returned to her room, eager to see her diorama again. A sinking feeling gripped her body. The diorama, her masterpiece, now lay shattered and scattered. It was as if a storm had swept through the room. All her hard work was in pieces.

Tears welled in her eyes. She knelt among the ruins, picking up the broken pieces. "I can't believe it... I worked so hard on this. It's all gone..."

* * *

Oscar and Bubba continued their search for adventure throughout the house. Their hearts raced with the thrill of discovery. Their curiosity led them down the hallway. Their playful footsteps echoed in anticipation. This led them straight into their parents' room. There, another surprise awaited them.

A pile of colorful blankets lay stacked on the bed.

Oscar exclaimed with excitement, "Look, Bubba! Let's make an epic fort!"

Bubba barked in agreement, wagging his tail furiously.

Without a second thought, they pounced on the blankets. They pulled them apart, throwing them in every direction.

Over the next few minutes, Oscar laid out all the cushions and pillows he could find. He built a long tunnel leading to a huge open space. Oscar then strung fairy lights over the fort's walls, giving it a magical glow.

The room was transformed into a wonderland. The two friends lost themselves in the excitement of it all.

The game of chase that followed only increased their happiness. Oscar and Bubba darted through the maze of blankets. But all good things must come to an end. Soon they tumbled out of the fort, breathless.

As they caught their breath, Oscar heard footsteps approaching. It was Mom! Acting quickly, they jumped out the window and into the garden.

By the time Mom came in, they had disappeared.

* * *

Mom entered, surveying the chaotic scene before her. The blankets lay in disarray, and the room was a jumbled mess.

She sighed. "What happened in here?"

The joy and excitement that had once filled the room were a distant memory. All that remained was a sense of loss and disappointment.

* * *

The rain finally stopped. Oscar and Bubba were delighted to feel the warmth of the sun on their faces. They enjoyed the fresh air, their laughter echoing loudly.

They eventually went back into the house. They were so caught up in the fun that they forgot to wipe their feet.

*Plop! Plop! Plop!*

They stomped in, leaving a trail of muddy footprints behind them. The floor that Mom had mopped that morning was filthy.

They were just about to go to Oscar's room when they heard a voice.

"That's it!" Mom cried.

They turned around to find a red-faced Mom staring at the muddy footprints. Even more concerning was the sight of a tearful Emma hugging her leg.

The image tugged at Oscar's heart.

Oscar approached them cautiously.

"M-Mom, what happened?" Oscar stammered, his voice full of guilt.

Mom sighed. "Oscar, your sister is upset because of what happened with her diorama. It was something she worked hard on, and it got damaged."

A wave of regret washed over Oscar at his mother's words. He had never intended to cause harm. He just wanted to have fun. Yet, he now realized the weight of his actions and the effect they had on those he cared about.

Bubba nuzzled against Emma's leg, offering a wordless apology.

When Oscar finally found the courage to speak, his voice shook. "I...I... Please don't be sad! I...promise to help fix everything. I promise!"

"What do you say, honey?" Mom asked, tapping on Emma's shoulder.

Emma sniffed but still gave a slight nod.

Oscar's heart swelled with gratitude.

Together, Oscar and Emma sat side by side, their hands working to repair the diorama.

Meanwhile, their mom guided Bubba over to a stack of blankets. He helped by eagerly bringing new blankets to replace the ones that needed to be washed.

Once Oscar was done helping his sister, he and Mom mopped the floor together. He saw how much effort and love his mom and sister had put into their work. He should've been careful. He should've respected their hard work more.

As they all sat down, Oscar felt the true weight of his actions. "Mom, Emma, I really am sorry about what I did today," he said, looking down at his hands.

"Oh, honey." Mom put an arm around his shoulders and pulled him closer. "We forgive you. Don't we?" she said, looking in Emma's direction.

Emma didn't say anything at first. She simply left the room but returned a few moments later.

"Wanna play with me?" Emma asked with a cheeky smile as she revealed the diorama hidden behind her back. Oscar smiled.

In that tender moment, the family learned a valuable lesson. They learned to respect others' belongings. A simple act of asking could have prevented all the heartbreak. They found the beauty of forgiveness and the strength in fixing what had been broken.

Remember, love and hope are powerful forces that can help us overcome mistakes and grow together as a family.

How can you show respect for others' belongings?

How can forgiveness and empathy make relationships stronger?

## CHAPTER THREE

# The Compassionate Duo

Oscar and Bubba were playing in their backyard, enjoying the sun, when Bubba accidentally stepped on a sharp rock hidden in the grass. He let out a whimper of surprise. The poor dog's paw was hurt, leaving him in a lot of pain.

Oscar's eyes widened with concern. "Oh no, Bubba! Are you okay?"

Bubba's ears drooped. He let out a soft whine. It was clear that Bubba's paw hurt a lot.

Oscar swiftly turned on his heels and ran inside. He found Dad in the living room, reading a book.

"Dad, Dad!" Oscar called breathlessly. "Bubba hurt his paw! We need your help!"

Dad closed his book, his face full of concern. He rushed to follow Oscar outside. He sat next to Bubba and examined the injured paw.

"Don't worry, Oscar," Dad said coolly. "I'll take care of Bubba."

Oscar watched as Dad cleaned the wound and wrapped a strip of gauze around it. He noted everything, seeing Dad's movements.

With Bubba's paw bandaged, Dad turned his attention to Oscar. He knelt to his son's level, their eyes meeting.

"Oscar," Dad began. "Bubba needs more than just physical care. He needs your love and compassion to help him feel better."

"I'll take care of Bubba, Dad. I'll show him plenty of love," Oscar declared, his voice determined.

Dad smiled warmly. "I know you will, my dear. You have a big heart."

With that, Dad gently carried Bubba inside the house. Oscar watched his father, feeling a mix of excitement and responsibility settle within him.

Dad set Bubba down on a cushion and then left to do his chores. Oscar carefully looked at his best friend. Bubba's eyes were bulging with sadness. Oscar simply couldn't bear to see him that way. So, he decided to go with the first idea that popped into his mind.

"You'll be smiling in no time, Bubba, just you wait!" Oscar said.

Oscar gathered all of Bubba's favorite treats and snacks. Then, he spread out a mat in front of the window, right in the warm sunlight. Next, he arranged the treats in a tempting display.

"Bubba, look! A special spot just for you!" Oscar announced.

Bubba's eyes lit up, and he wagged his tail. But he hesitated to stand. Oscar noticed and gently lifted him onto the mat. Bubba's eyes showed gratitude, but his tail drooped. He let out a soft whimper.

"Bubba, are you not excited about the treats?" Oscar asked, puzzled.

He then saw why Bubba couldn't enjoy them. Sitting on the thin mat on the hard floor made his injured paw hurt more.

"Oh, I didn't think about that, Bubba. I'm sorry." Oscar gently cradled Bubba's body in his arms and put him back on his plush cushion.

"Don't worry!" Oscar said, raising his hands. "I'll find something else to make you happy!"

Oscar quickly came up with another plan. He gathered all of Bubba's squeaky toys and created a parade.

"Look, Bubba! It's a toy parade just for you!" Oscar exclaimed. He even made trumpet and drum sounds.

Bubba barked happily and tried to wag his tail. Yet, his paw throbbed, making him wince. He tried to play, but his excitement faded quickly.

Oscar frowned, noticing that Bubba's eyes were still sad. "Bubba, I thought the toy parade would make you happy," Oscar said, kneeling beside him.

Bubba gave him a gentle nuzzle. His eyes said thanks, but he didn't want to play.

"I'll think of something else for us to do!" Oscar told Bubba as he picked up all the toys. He still remembered how hard Mom had worked to clean the room. It wouldn't be fair to leave a mess here. Not even if he was trying to make Bubba happy.

Once he had put everything in place, he searched for another idea. Oscar was determined to see Bubba's tail wag again.

He grabbed his guitar and began strumming cheerful tunes. "Let's have a sing-along, Bubba! Music can make anyone feel better!" Oscar declared, singing his heart out.

Bubba's ears perked up, and he tried to join in the fun. But as he moved to the music, his hurt paw made him stumble.

"Ummh! Ummh!" Bubba let out a pained sound.

Oscar stopped playing at once, realizing his mistake.

"Oh, Bubba, I'm so sorry! I didn't realize dancing would hurt you," Oscar said softly. "I'm really sorry, Bubba. None of my plans seem to be working..." His voice was tinged with regret.

Dad, who had overheard the conversation, entered the room. He went to Oscar and Bubba, a warm smile on his face.

"What's with the long face, Oscar?" Dad asked.

Oscar was ready to burst. He didn't wait a single moment before telling Dad everything.

"But you see, nothing's worked." Oscar huffed at the end, slapping his hands to his sides. "There isn't much we can do since Bubba's hurt."

Dad, who had been listening attentively, gave Oscar a soft smile. "I think you're now starting to understand what compassion is."

"What do you mean?" Oscar scratched his cheek.

"Bubba being hurt is compassion?"

"No, but you realizing that he's hurt is compassion," Dad replied.

"Ummm...so you mean to say I should make my choices by keeping in mind that Bubba's hurt?" Oscar asked with a slight tilt to his head.

"Right!" Dad smiled, snapping his fingers. "We call that putting ourselves in other people's shoes."

"You mean put myself in Bubba's paws," Oscar laughed.

"Well, you could say that too," Dad agreed, chuckling.

A newfound purpose grew in Oscar's eyes at his dad's words. He wanted to make Bubba feel happy and loved. A smile spread across his face.

"I have an idea, Dad!"

With his plan in motion, Oscar carried Bubba outside. Oscar settled Bubba in the soft grass beside him. Bubba's tail wagged with excitement as he enjoyed nature.

They watched Oscar's sister, Emma, dart across the yard, her laughter ringing. Her excitement brought joy to both Oscar and Bubba.

Mom and Dad, having finished their work, joined them outside. They smiled warmly at Oscar, proud of his compassionate act.

Bubba turned his head and gently licked Oscar's cheek. It was his way of thanking him. Oscar beamed, feeling beyond happy. In that moment, he knew he had made a difference in Bubba's world.

Imagine how Bubba must have felt when Oscar sat with him in the cozy grass! How would you feel if someone showed you such superhero kindness?

What can we learn from Oscar's amazing actions toward Bubba?

## CHAPTER FOUR

# The Enchanted Afternoon

As quickly as she could, little Emma joined the line for the bus. Right behind her was her best friend, Josephine. Today was the first time Josephine was coming over to Emma's house.

"I can't wait until we get to your house," Josephine said.

"Oh, me neither," Emma exclaimed. "I've got so much planned for us!"

Finally, the girls reached Emma's home.

As they approached the front door, Emma took a deep breath. She turned to Josephine, her voice a whisper of excitement. "Are you ready, Josephine?" she asked.

Josephine nodded, her heart thumping with joy. "Yes, I'm ready!"

With that, Emma pushed open the door. Their hearts

were brimming with hope for the adventure that lay ahead.

Together they bounded inside the house. Just as Emma had expected, the smell of freshly baked cookies welcomed them. The two friends practically floated to the kitchen, their mouths watering.

"Plan number one, Josephine: The Great Cookie Party!"

Their laughter filled the room as they reached for the cookies. But the tray suddenly slipped.

## *CRASH!*

It fell to the floor with a heartbreaking *bang*. Emma's eyes widened in shock, and Josephine gasped.

They were still dealing with what had happened when Bubba suddenly entered the kitchen. The sugar-loving dog bolted toward the fallen cookies.

"Noooooo!" Emma cried. But it was too late.

Bubba had already started chomping down on them.

Tears welled in Emma's eyes. The sadness felt like a heavy cloud over her heart. "Oh no, Josephine, our cookies... They're gone, just like that."

Josephine's eyes twinkled with mischief as she patted Bubba's head. "Well, Bubba definitely liked them!"

Emma's pout deepened, "But Josephine, those cookies were going to be the best part of our day."

Determined to save their afternoon, they went out in the garden. There, they saw Gamma with some special supplies. Emma had invited her grandmother to come over today. She wanted Gamma to teach them how to paint on clay pottery.

The girls' faces glowed with excitement. They dipped their brushes into different colors, creating magic. "Plan number two, Josephine: Enchanted Pottery Art!"

The only thing they didn't pay attention to was Luna. The curious cat sat on the far side of the table where they worked, her eyes fixed on the colors.

"You're both doing so well," Gamma said, impressed with their art. "They look amazing!"

It wasn't just the girls having fun playing with colors. Luna, the playful trickster, couldn't resist the swirling colors either. With a flick of her tail, she sent the paints toppling over, splattering the pottery the girls had just finished.

Gasps escaped from both of them, their eyes wide with disbelief. "Luna, no! Look what you've done!" Josephine exclaimed.

Emma's shoulders slumped. A heavy sigh left her lips. "Our pottery... It's ruined!"

Seeing Emma's sad expression, Josephine tried to make her smile. "I guess Luna wanted to be an artist too!"

Emma nodded, chucking a little. "Yeah... It seems like nothing's working. But don't worry, okay? I have one more idea. We can watch our favorite new movie!"

The girls ran to the living room, ready for a cozy movie. Emma picked up the remote, her excitement building. "Okay, let's get this movie started!"

She pressed the play button, but the screen remained black. Emma's heart sank as she understood what was wrong. "Oh no, I think Oscar forgot to download the movie."

Sitting on the edge of the couch, Emma and Josephine exchanged glances. Their eyes held a mix of sorrow and disappointment.

But then, as the sun began to set, Emma's gaze brightened. She couldn't give up.

"I know our day didn't go like we thought. But Josephine, we can't let that beat us. It's the first time you've come to my house. I can't let you leave until we have some fun!"

Side by side, they thought of some more fun ideas. They turned socks into crazy puppets and put on a puppet show. Then, they wore Emma's mom's old hats and twirled around the room. The girls even held a dance party under the shade of the apple tree. They spun and twirled, singing their hearts out.

As the day came to an end, Emma and Josephine flopped onto the grass. They were breathless from laughter. Emma wiped a tear from her eye. A tear not of sadness but of joy.

"Josephine, you know what? Even though the cookies and our art *and* our movie got ruined, today was still... AMAZING!" Emma said in wonder.

Josephine grinned. "So true! Together, we made the day fun."

As Emma went to sleep that night, she realized she had learned a very important lesson: never give up hope. Life can be full of surprises, both good and bad. Yet, she had the power to change even the bad ones into something good, if she only stayed hopeful.

What did you learn from Emma's story?

How can hope make our lives better?

Can you think of a time when hope made a difference for you?

What are some things you can do when you feel hopeless in order to be hopeful again?

## CHAPTER FIVE

# The Crown of True Friendship

Once there was a bright Kingdom of Friendship. It lay within the walls of a bustling schoolyard. Two young girls named Emma and Josephine were known as its rulers.

Emma imagined herself as a regal queen. Josephine often dreamt of being the queen's cherished princess.

But one sunny afternoon, as the two gathered at the playground, a sudden twist happened. A fight broke out.

In seconds, the kingdom was clouded by sadness. Both the rulers, it seemed, wanted the same thing.

"I should be the queen today," Josephine declared, her voice filled with purpose.

Emma's face scrunched up, her tongue sticking out playfully. "No way! I want to be the queen! I thought of the kingdom first!"

A frown tugged at Josephine's lips. "But I want to be the queen sometimes too. Can't we both be queens?"

Emma's cheeks flushed as she crossed her arms. "No! There can only be one queen, and that's me!"

Emma was unable to see past her own stubborn wishes. "I don't want to be your friend anymore!" Emma declared.

Josephine gasped in shock. Large tears welled in her eyes. With a broken heart, she turned and ran, not wanting to see Emma.

Emma, too caught up in her anger, was left alone on the swing set. Swinging back and forth, she began to realize the weight of her words. She no longer had a best friend.

As the school day passed, Emma's heart felt heavy. She wanted to apologize, but something kept her away from Josephine. Fate, however, had other plans in store.

Emma entered the classroom, her footsteps hesitant. She walked to the desk she shared with Josephine. A space once filled with laughter now only held silence.

Emma slid into her seat, keeping her back to Josephine. She shifted uncomfortably. Emma missed her friend, but she also didn't want to talk to her.

Josephine's voice broke the awkward silence. "Emma, do you have an extra pencil? I forgot mine."

Emma's eyes stayed fixed on her textbook. Her voice was like a robot as she replied, "Here." She rolled the pencil across the desk without meeting Josephine's eyes. She did not say another word.

Josephine's smile slowly disappeared. Having Emma avoid her hurt more than any sharp words ever could.

Soon the bell rang, signaling the end of the school day. Emma and Josephine found themselves side by side once again, this time on the bus.

Emma chose a seat on one side of the aisle, while Josephine settled on the other. Their eyes met briefly, but Emma quickly looked away.

Her heart tugged with both regret and longing. She wanted to apologize. But pride and stubbornness stopped her.

\*\*\*

The next day, Emma found herself on the playground again. Sitting on the swing, her heart missed Josephine.

They usually had so much fun playing hide-and-seek. Then, when they'd get tired, they would take turns on the swings. They also loved pretending to be fairies. Fairies who flew from fluffy cloud to fluffy cloud. There was never a dull moment with Josephine around.

"I miss her so much!" Emma said out loud. This was a truth she had been hiding from for the past day.

"But I've hurt her so much," Emma said, looking at the spot where she had said those mean words to Josephine. "She'll never forgive me..."

A sudden hopelessness overtook Emma. She still felt a little angry over their fight. Yet, a much bigger part of her wanted to fix their friendship. She looked up at all the kids around her. They all had someone to play with. Someone to share secrets with.

Emma once had all of that too, but now it was gone.

"No!" Emma quickly shook her head. "Josephine's my best friend. I want her back!"

Inspired by those words, Emma felt a spark of courage within her. She stood up from the swing, knowing what she had to do.

Emma spotted Josephine near the sandbox. Her heart raced as she trudged closer.

"Josephine," she began slowly, "I'm sorry for what I said yesterday. I never want to lose you as my friend."

Josephine turned to face Emma, her eyes full of hurt. Yet, slowly the hurt was pushed away by a smile. A small smile, but one that Emma knew was real.

"I forgive you!"

As soon as those words left Josephine's mouth, Emma couldn't hold herself back. She pulled her dear friend in for a hug.

"I missed you so much," Emma mumbled.

Josephine tightened the hug. "Me too!"

As they pulled away, Emma's heart swelled with warmth. She looked into Josephine's eyes and smiled. "Josephine, you're right. Let's play. But this time, let's both be queens."

Josephine's face lit up with joy, and she nodded eagerly. "I love that idea, Emma!"

And so, the Kingdom of Friendship was restored, all because the girls had learned the importance of forgiveness. They now knew about the beauty of sharing the crown of friendship. In friendship and forgiveness, the hearts of both queens found peace.

What have you
learned from
this story?

How would you
define friendship?

Share your
thoughts and let
your imagination soar!

## CHAPTER SIX

# The Tower of Hope

*T*he sheriff stood tall in the middle of the street. His old cowboy hat sat low on his head. His face was full of purpose.

*In front of him, a rowdy gang of sheep narrowed their eyes. Ready to destroy…*

"Ahhh!" came a cry.

Startled, Oscar looked up. The toy cowboy and sheep slipped from his hand. In his imaginary world, the herd of sheep hadn't yet attacked. So, where had the cry come from?

Oscar then realized the sound had come from his sister, Emma. Emma, too, was busy playing with her own toys a few steps away in the living room. Judging by the frown on her lips, things weren't going her way.

Shrugging, Oscar turned back to his own toys.

*The sheriff's hand rested on the rim of his hat. His eyes locked onto the sheep. He was ready to face them.*

"Noooooo!!!!"

Again, Oscar's fictional world was shattered. He huffed.

"What's wrong, Emma?" Oscar sighed.

Emma looked up. "I've been trying all day to get this tower to stand, but it just keeps falling over!"

Oscar was annoyed. But he could also tell that the tower mattered to her.

"It's okay," Oscar said. He picked up a Lego and offered it to Emma. "I know you can do it if you don't give up."

Emma bit her lip, not feeling all that confident. Nevertheless, she decided to give it another try.

Oscar nodded. Yet, his attention had already gone back to his own toys. He was on an important mission.

Mom, who had been watching them, came to sit next to Oscar. She offered him a smile. "I'm really proud of how you tried to encourage Emma to not give up," she said, ruffling his hair. "But Oscar, can you show Emma a little more kindness? Maybe lend her a hand?"

Oscar's brows drew together in a frown. His toys called out to him. He wanted to play with them badly. But then Oscar looked at Emma. Her tower had fallen down once again. This time she didn't even bother complaining. Emma simply flung a handful of Legos at the wall in anger.

Oscar sighed. "I guess I could help her a little later, but right now, I'm in the middle of something."

He looked at his sister, who was still fuming over the Legos. He remembered how helpless he'd felt when Bubba was wounded, and he couldn't do anything to ease the dog's pain. He felt a twinge of sympathy for Emma. Perhaps this was his chance to help her out. And so, a minute later, Oscar found himself sitting beside Emma.

"Take a deep breath, Emma," he said, his calm voice. "Inhale slowly and then exhale. Let all that anger flow out."

Emma copied her brother. Her small chest rising and falling with his.

With newfound peace, Oscar turned his attention to the tower. He showed her how to start with a strong foundation. This was important if she didn't want the tower to fall.

Side by side, they built the tower, working together. With Oscar's help, Emma made the tower taller than ever.

As the final block found its place, Emma's eyes shimmered with pride. She flung her arms around Oscar.

"Thank you," she whispered. "I couldn't have done it without you."

Oscar's eyes softened, his heart swelling. In that moment, he understood the true power of kindness. It could make even the saddest heart smile.

"You're welcome, Emma," he replied, his cheeks turning red. "Sometimes, all it takes is a little kindness to make a big difference."

What did Oscar do
to help his sister,
Emma, when she was
frustrated?

Why do you think
it's important to be patient
when things don't
go as planned?

Can you think
of a time when someone
showed you kindness?
How did it make you feel?

## CHAPTER SEVEN

# Toto and the Mysterious Weekend

One Friday afternoon, Emma skipped home from school. Her hands clutched a small container with a surprise inside.

"Hurry up, Oscar!" Emma called in excitement. She wanted to zoom down the street to their house. Yet, Emma knew she had to cross the road with her brother.

She looked down at the box resting in her hand, carefully balancing it, trying her best not to jostle it. Emma had an important task.

As she entered the house, her eyes sparkled. Luna and Bubba both entered the hallway. The cat and dog, too, sensed something new in the air. Even Dad looked up from his book with interest.

"Guess what, everyone? We have a special visitor this weekend!" Emma exclaimed.

"What's all the excitement about, Emma?" Dad asked, raising an eyebrow.

Emma grinned. "I brought home Toto, the school lizard, for the weekend! We get to take care of him as part of a project. Isn't that cool?"

Just then, Mom entered the room "You know, Emma," she began, "helping with two pets can be quite a handful. Are you sure you're up for it?"

"Don't worry, Mom. I take care of Luna all the time. I'll be an expert at taking care of Toto too!" Emma replied.

With her parents' approval, Emma bounded up the stairs. The box was still cradled gently in her hands. She entered her room and placed Toto on her desk. As she opened the lid, Toto peered out. The lizard's tiny eyes looked at his new surroundings.

Emma whispered, "Get ready, Toto. Luna is going to be so curious about you!"

The cat hopped onto the desk, her eyes curiously looking over at Toto. Toto, on the other hand, licked his lips. A silent hello in lizard language.

Meanwhile, Bubba wagged his tail outside Emma's door. He, too, wanted to meet the mysterious Toto.

Carefully, Emma fed Toto crackers with some water. She then set up a mini obstacle course on her desk. She planned to be the best lizard caretaker in her entire class.

"Emma, there's a call for you!" Emma's mom announced from downstairs.

Her heart fluttered with excitement as she heard those words. She turned to Toto, a wide smile lighting up her face.

"That must be Josephine!" Emma exclaimed. "I'll be right back, Toto. Don't go anywhere!"

Emma hurried out of her room, leaving the door slightly ajar. Toto, curious about his new surroundings, began to explore. Luna, too, stepped closer to Toto, curious to learn more about him.

Suddenly, with a burst of energy, she jumped at Toto. Scared, Toto scurried away, his small body darting off the desk to hide under Emma's bed.

Meanwhile, Emma returned to her room holding her mom's tablet. She was on a video call with Josephine. Eagerly glancing at her desk, Emma's eyes searched for Toto's green presence. Her cheerful expression quickly changed into one of worry.

Toto was nowhere to be found.

Panic gripped Emma's heart as she started looking around. "Josephine!" she cried. "Toto's missing!"

Josephine's face mirrored Emma's distress. "Emma, what happened?"

Tears welled in Emma's eyes as she struggled to find the words. "I don't know, Josephine! I left Toto outside his cage... Now he's gone!"

"Oh no, Emma! You have to find him!" Josephine said.

Emma's cries for help soon reached her parents' ears. Mom and Dad rushed upstairs.

"What happened, sweetheart?" Dad asked, his voice filled with worry.

Emma sniffled. "Toto...he's gone! What if he's lost forever?"

Mom knelt down beside Emma, wrapping her arms around her. "It's all right, Emma. We'll find him. Let's look together."

Mom, Dad, and Emma looked through the room. They searched everywhere. Emma's tears slowly dried up. With all of them searching together, she had hope of finding Toto.

Suddenly, Luna came out from beneath the bed. Her tail held high and proud. There, hanging from her mouth by his tiny tail, was Toto. Emma gasped as relief washed over her.

"Luna! Drop him!" Emma pleaded, her voice filled with urgency.

Luna obediently let go of Toto, who fell into Emma's hands.

"Oh, Toto! You're safe!" Emma whispered, hugging the little lizard.

Mom and Dad sighed in relief too.

Dad opened his mouth to speak, his voice kind but stern. "Emma—" he said, but Emma cut him off.

"I know," Emma said in a low voice, looking down at her feet. "I should have been more careful. The entire class trusted me with him."

"That's right, my dear," Mom chimed in. "Accidents like this can easily happen."

Emma looked up at her mom. "As Dad always says, we should learn from our mistakes and try not to repeat them."

She looked back at Toto. "Mom, Dad, I promise I'll be more responsible. From now on, I'll always keep an eye on him."

Dad smiled warmly. "That's all we ask, sweetheart."

Together, they placed Toto back into his box.

At dinner, Mom and Dad shared their own funny pet stories. Emma and Oscar laughed as they listened. But the entire time, Emma kept one eye on Toto. She had promised to be more responsible. She was going to take that promise seriously.

What did Emma learn about taking care of pets?

Can you think of a time when you had to take responsibility for something important?

If you have pets, how do you show love and care for them?

# CHAPTER EIGHT

# The Gratitude Diary

Emma dashed through the front door after school and found her parents in the kitchen. She plopped a writing journal on the kitchen table.

"What's this?" asked her dad. He slid his work to one side and gave Emma his full attention.

"This," she declared, "is a gratitude journal. My teacher gave it to me at school!"

Her father's brow arched with interest. "So, what's gratitude?"

Emma reached for a chocolate chip cookie from the jar nearby. Taking a bite, she paused for a moment. She recalled what her teacher had explained in class. "Gratitude is when you feel happy and thankful for what you have."

"And how does that journal fit into all of this?"

Emma's eyes gleamed. "Each day, I'll find at least three things to be thankful for and write them down here," she explained, drumming her fingers against the journal.

Emma dashed into her room. Finding her purple glitter pen, she flipped the journal open.

After the talk with her parents, she knew exactly what to write. She was grateful for the best parents in the entire world! Emma quickly wrote down those feelings.

*What else am I grateful for?* Emma thought, tapping the pen against her chin.

She spotted a picture taken of her and Oscar playing on the beach. Emma laughed at that memory. *He can be annoying at times. But I'm grateful to have an older brother too.*

Emma had just finished writing when she was nearly toppled off her chair. Bubba jumped right on top of her, licking Emma's face, a sign of his deep love for her.

"I haven't forgotten you either," Emma said, scratching the dog behind the ear. "I'm thankful to have you as well."

Satisfied, Emma closed her journal and set it aside. She finished just in time for dinner.

Downstairs, Emma was surprised to find that her grandma had come over.

"Gammaaaa!" Emma yelled, running to give her grandma a hug.

As they all sat down, Emma excitedly told Gamma about her homework.

"Actually, I just finished my first entry in the journal," Emma said. "Would you like to have a look?"

"Only if it's okay with you, honey," her grandma replied with a sweet smile.

Emma didn't wait another second. She left the kitchen only to return a minute later. She gave her journal to Gamma, her heart full of pride.

Gamma gently took the journal and read it. "Oh, my loving child, this is beautiful."

Emma beamed. "Thank you, Gamma," she replied, her voice filled with gratitude. "Writing in my journal makes me realize how lucky I am."

Gamma nodded, her gaze soft. "Yes, my dear, expressing gratitude is beautiful. But let me share a secret with you."

Emma's curiosity stirred as she leaned closer. "What is it, Gamma?"

"Showing gratitude is far better than just the words we write or say," she explained. "It's all about taking action."

Emma's brows pulled together with curiosity. She looked at her journal that lay closed in Gamma's lap. Then her eyes moved up to her parents eating dinner nearby. She caught sight of Oscar eating right next to her at the table.

*What if I found a way to show gratitude to all of them too?* Emma thought excitedly to herself.

"Gamma," Emma spoke up. "Do you think I can show gratitude to someone by doing things that make them happy?"

"I don't see why not," Gamma smiled, sipping water.

Emma's heart swelled with gratitude for Gamma's guidance.

Dinner was over. Yet, the aroma of a delicious meal still lingered in the air. With Emma's stomach full, she looked at her mom with gratitude.

"Dinner was delicious, Mom," Emma exclaimed. "Thank you for all that you do."

As Mom and Dad rose from their seats, Emma's mind

raced with a brilliant idea. In a swift motion, she jumped to action.

"Wait, Mom!" she called. "I want to help clean up."

Mom sat back down, her eyes wide with surprise. Dad beamed with pride at Emma. Oscar, inspired by Emma, joined in too.

Together, Emma and Oscar swiftly cleared the table. Plates clinked and utensils clattered.

As Emma finished, she saw Bubba trying to reach for his favorite toy. Because of his recently injured paw, he couldn't get it. Emma hugged Bubba and gave him the toy. But she didn't stop there. Running quickly, she went to the lounge where they kept a basket full of Bubba's toys. Emma picked up the ones she knew Bubba played with the most. When she laid them in front of Bubba, he gave her the sweetest smile.

Back in the kitchen, Mom was cutting into the apple pie she had made that day. One of the pieces happened to be larger than the rest. At first, Emma wanted that for herself. But then she remembered how much Oscar loved Mom's pies.

The choice became very simple after that. Emma grabbed the plate. She put a big dollop of whipped cream on top (just how Oscar liked it) and gave it to her brother.

"Wow!" Oscar said, pleasantly surprised. "Thank you!"

"What a dear girl you are," Gamma said, taking hold of Emma's hand.

"I just wanted to show you guys that I mean it when I say I'm thankful for you," Emma said in a small voice, her cheeks turning pink.

"And we're thankful to have you, honey," Mom said. She then gave Emma a piece of pie cut into the shape of a heart.

Emma's eyes sparkled as she took her plate. She placed a kiss on her mom's cheek. "Love you, Mom!"

Emma was glad she didn't stop at just writing about gratitude. She was happy to have shown everyone how thankful she was to have them. And in the end, that's what really matters. Why? Because actions always speak louder than words.

What have you
learned from Emma's
gratitude Journal
project?

How can you show
gratitude in your own life?
How does expressing gratitude
make you feel?

Can you think of a time
when someone showed
gratitude toward you?
How did it make you feel?

## CHAPTER NINE

# Oscar's Sharing Adventure

"Oscar, come here, please," his grandma called. "The people are hungry!"

Looking up from his task, Oscar clucked his tongue. "Coming, Gamma!"

It was a slightly chilly Saturday morning. Oscar and Gamma were gathered for a special event at the park. A local charity had helped put together a party for all the town's seniors. Their mission was to help the senior citizens have fun. Oscar and Gamma were handling the food station. Gamma had even made her famous soup for the occasion.

"There, we can open now!" Gamma smiled.

As soon as Oscar put up the "Open" sign, a huge group of people gathered. He and his grandma stood side by side at their soup station. Gamma poured warm soup into bowls. Everyone loved their soup so much, they had sold out in an hour!

After all the hard work, Oscar finally sat down with his own bowl of soup. It was the last bowl of soup that was left. He was just about to take the first spoonful when...

"Excuse me?"

Oscar looked up to find an elderly lady standing next to the stall. She looked to be around Gamma's age but seemed very weak. When she pointed her finger at the soup, it shook. And Oscar could tell it was hard for her to stand.

"Is there any soup left?" she asked.

Oscar looked from his bowl of soup over to the pot he knew was empty back at the stall. There was only one choice. Yet, it was a hard one.

"Please have a seat," Oscar said, helping the lady. "I'll bring you your soup."

Oscar sat the lady down on a bench. Then he quickly left to bring her what would have been his bowl of soup.

"Enjoy!" Oscar smiled as he laid it in front of her.

In a soft voice, the lady said, "Child, your heart is full of warmth and kindness. Thank you so much!"

Oscar blushed. He felt as though his heart was wrapped in a cozy hug. He nodded in thanks, then skipped back to his stall. He wanted this happiness to last. There was only one way to do that. He was going to find more ways to help people.

* * *

The next day at school, Oscar saw another person who needed help. It was recess. Kids were running all around.

"Please don't fall, please don't fall," Oscar heard Mrs. Johnson plead.

Her small arms were full of heavy books. It was clear she was having a hard time.

Oscar didn't hesitate.

"I'm here to help, Mrs. Johnson," Oscar declared.

He caught one book just as it was about to fall. Seeing him, all of Oscar's friends were inspired too. One by one, they went up to Mrs. Johnson and took a few books. Oscar and his friends felt like knights on a mission. Their gleaming armor was made of kindness.

* * *

Later that day, another great idea came to Oscar. He was going to give his neighborhood friends a surprise.

Reaching into his pocket, he took out some coins. It was money he had been saving for a week now. With a heart full of love, he bought small gifts for his friends.

A shiny marble for Alex, a sparkly sticker for Lily, and a bouncy ball for Max. When Oscar gave away the gifts, a ripple of kindness spread.

His friends thanked Oscar. They, too, were inspired to do something kind.

"Here, you can use my crayon," Alex said, extending his favorite blue crayon to Oscar.

Lily, who never shared her cookies, opened her lunch box and put it in the middle of the table. "You guys can have some too!"

Max, on the other hand, decided to entertain everyone. He told a lot of jokes that day. And even though most of the jokes weren't very good, all their friends laughed. But most of all, it was Oscar who felt happy. His one good deed had multiplied into many. They had made a circle of sharing. Four beautiful hearts joined by kindness.

* * *

When Gamma came over that weekend, Oscar told her about all the good he had done.

"I'm proud of you, Oscar," Gamma said.

It was then that Oscar's eyes fell on Emma's toys. A new idea came to him. "Gamma, Emma, how about we donate some of our toys to kids who don't have as many as we do?"

"I like that idea!" Emma brightened. "We could ask other kids in the neighborhood to donate too."

So, with hearts full of purpose, they decided to knock on their neighbors' doors. They shared their mission with everyone.

Mr. Jenkins donated a colorful puzzle. Mrs. Thompson gave away a soft bear. All the kids gave away a few prized toys. Oscar's heart swelled with pride. He felt like a superhero. His power was kindness.

After days of planning, the big day of the event finally came. The entire neighborhood buzzed with excitement. Everyone talked about what they were going to donate.

However, as Oscar looked at his toys, he felt uncertain. His favorite toys were like old friends. He didn't want to part with them. At once, Emma noticed something was wrong.

With a smile, she asked, "What's wrong, Oscar?"

Oscar hesitated before admitting, "I want to share my toys, Emma. But...I also love them."

Emma's eyes twinkled as she replied, "I know how you feel. I didn't want to give Mr. Cuddles away either."

"Wait, what?!" Oscar paused in amazement. "You donated *Mr. Cuddles*?"

"Yup!" Emma nodded.

Oscar couldn't believe his ears. Mr. Cuddles was Emma's favorite teddy bear. Emma never slept without him.

"But you know what?" Emma continued. "I forgot how sad I felt when I saw the girl who had gotten Mr. Cuddles. I think that's what sharing is all about."

Oscar thought about Emma's words. She was right. Oscar remembered all the times he had shared things with other kids—how happy it had made them. Their happiness, in turn, had made him feel happy.

So, Oscar ran up to his room. There he picked out a handful of his cherished toys. He was going to donate them. He thought he was going to feel sad. However, he felt lighter after making that decision.

As the event unfolded, kids of all ages gathered. Their eyes glowed as they received their toys. Their smiles

shined brighter than the summer sun. Oscar watched, his heart swelling with happiness. He realized that sharing wasn't about the toys themselves. The important thing was the joy they brought to others.

In the end, Oscar walked home happy. He was going to miss his toys for sure. But he knew they would make some other kids even happier. And in that moment, their happiness meant more to him.

How did Oscar's kindness create a chain reaction among his friends?
Can you think of a time when you shared something?

What's a way you can share kindness with someone today?

## CHAPTER TEN

# EMMA'S BRAVE GARDEN QUEST

"Ooohhhh! That's so prettyyyy!!!"

Emma and her mom were in the garden planting the new flowers they had bought. Together, they dug holes for the flowers and carefully placed the plants into them.

"Careful, honey." Mom guided Emma as she placed a flower in the soil. Emma felt like an artist. The garden was their beautiful painting.

Yet, there was something that made Emma feel uneasy—caterpillars. They were crawling all over the leaves, munching on them like green explorers. To Emma, they looked strange and wiggly. She didn't like them one bit.

Emma watched as their little legs moved in rhythm. She wrinkled her nose and said, "I don't like caterpillars."

Her mom smiled kindly. "You know, Emma," she said, "caterpillars are just little creatures trying to find their way." She placed her hand under a leaf, and a caterpillar climbed on it. "And you know, they don't stay caterpillars forever. They turn into beautiful butterflies!"

Emma's eyes widened in curiosity. "Really?"

"Yes, really," Mom replied, tapping her nose. "They look a little strange now. But they'll go on a magical journey. By the end of it, they'll become something amazing."

Emma tried to imagine it all. *A caterpillar turns into a colorful butterfly!* That made her feel a little better and less afraid of the tiny creepy crawlies.

"Caterpillars become butterflies," she whispered to herself.

But then, her mom said something different.

"Some caterpillars, however, turn into moths."

"What?" Emma's eyes widened. A shiver ran down her spine. She didn't like moths very much, either!

She tried to stay calm after that. She tried very hard. She moved away from where most of the caterpillars were and tried to finish up quickly.

But then she saw a caterpillar climbing on her hand. Emma left everything behind, shaking it off her hand and running into the house screaming.

Emma stayed so upset by it all, even Oscar noticed.

"What is it, Emma?" her brother asked. "I promise I didn't do anything this time."

Emma looked up from where she was having a tea party with a teddy bear. "I know you didn't..."

She took a deep breath and hugged the bear. "It's the caterpillars."

"What caterpillars?" Oscar laughed.

Emma poked her tongue out but continued. "In the garden," she said. "I need to stop being afraid of cater-pillars. What should I do?"

Oscar thought for a moment and then had an idea. He went to the garden and returned with a tiny cater-pillar on a leaf.

Sitting next to Emma, he said, "You can do this, Emma."

With a deep breath, Emma reached out a finger. But just as her finger got close, the caterpillar wiggled away.

"Ahhhhh!!!" Emma screamed. She felt like crying.

"Okay, okay, I'll put it back!" Oscar quickly ran to the garden.

Emma, on the other hand, was scared. Very scared. But that also made her feel mad at herself.

Oscar was back in no time. "You don't need to feel afraid anymore, Emma."

Emma sniffled and looked up at Oscar. "I just don't want to be a scaredy cat!"

Oscar stayed silent for a second and then said, "You know, Emma, being brave isn't about never feeling scared. You remember how scared I am of spiders, right?"

Emma nodded.

"Well, Alex brought his pet spider to school yesterday. In front of the whole class, I screamed at the top of my lungs when I saw it."

Emma covered her mouth. For Oscar to have screamed in front of everyone was a huge deal.

"But you know, by the end of the day, I faced my fear."

"How?!" Emma asked.

"Well, Alex loaned me his gloves. When I touched the spider wearing the gloves, I didn't feel as scared. I was brave enough to try touching the spider even though it scared me."

Emma wiped her tears and thought about what Oscar had said. She nodded, feeling a little better.

Oscar perked up. "Hey, I have an idea!" He found a pair of gloves and a hat. He helped Emma put them on.

"Now you have your superhero gear," he said with a wink.

Emma smiled and looked at the gloves. She felt stronger and ready to face her fear. With Oscar by her side and the gloves on her hands, Emma went back to the garden.

The caterpillars were still there. Yet, Emma felt ready. She watered the flowers and pulled up weeds. She even looked at the caterpillars from a safe distance. Her heart raced, but she stayed strong.

As the day went on, Emma learned something important: it was okay to be afraid sometimes. But she shouldn't let her fear stop her from doing something.

Emma smiled as she whispered to herself, "If caterpillars can become butterflies, I can become brave."

What things
scare you?

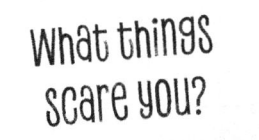

How do you feel
when you are afraid?

After listening to Emma's
story, do you think you can
face your fears too?

**Each book that we have published has a free audio version available.** To download the audiobook for *Stories About What's Important In Life,* **all you have to do is scan the QR code** or visit: www.littlebigpage.com/life

If you have any problems or questions, feel free to contact us at help@littlebigpage.com

# SADDLE UP FOR A SCHOOL YEAR WITH THE BEST CLASSMATES EVER: UNICORNS!

Made in United States
Orlando, FL
22 January 2025

57647448R00055